D1165562

REMARKABLE
**LGBTQ
LIVES**™

James
BALDWIN

GROUNDBREAKING AUTHOR AND CIVIL RIGHTS ACTIVIST

SUSAN HENNEBERG

ROSEN
PUBLISHING®

New York

James
BALDWIN

GROUNDBREAKING AUTHOR AND CIVIL RIGHTS ACTIVIST

Published in 2015 by The Rosen Publishing Group, Inc.
29 East 21st Street, New York, NY 10010

Library of Congress Cataloging-in-Publication Data

Henneberg, Susan, author.
James Baldwin/Susan Henneberg.—First Edition.
    pages cm.—(Remarkable LGBTQ lives)
Includes bibliographical references and index.
ISBN 978-1-4777-7897-5 (library bound)
1. Baldwin, James, 1924–1987—Juvenile literature. 2.
Authors, American—20th century—Biography—Juvenile
literature. 3. African American authors—Biography—
Juvenile literature. 4. Civil rights workers—United
States—Biography—Juvenile literature. I. Title.
PS3552.A45Z694 2015
818'.5409—dc23
[B]

                                    2014009638

Manufactured in China

CONTENTS

INTRO

According to biographer James Campbell, a reporter once asked James Baldwin how it felt starting out as a writer who was black, poor, and homosexual. "You must have thought, 'Gee, how disadvantaged can I get?'" Baldwin just smiled. "No," he said. "I think I hit the jackpot.'" What did he mean by that? The answer is in his writing. In essays, novels, and plays, he explores issues of race, sex, and class in America. What were obstacles to others were opportunities for him. Growing up as an African American in the middle part of the twentieth century was difficult. Being openly gay was subversive. Yet Baldwin used his complicated identity to write about themes that other writers avoided, such as interracial relationships and homosexuality. At the core of each piece of writing was Baldwin's belief about love.

James Baldwin was born in Harlem during the Harlem Renaissance. This period was known for an outpouring of the arts in the poorest part of New York City in the 1920s. He was the oldest of nine children. "I began plotting novels at about the time I learned to read," he wrote in *Collected Essays.* He also followed in his step-father's footsteps. He became a preacher at age fourteen in a local storefront church. It was during this time that he was figuring out his sexuality. By the time he was twenty, he thought of himself as homosexual.

James Baldwin worked tirelessly over a forty-year writing career to promote his message of tolerance and respect for African Americans and homosexuals.

This was a dangerous time for gay and lesbian people. Sex between same-gender adults was a crime in almost all states. Men and women were often fired from their jobs if they came out as gay or lesbian.

Baldwin was not able to afford college. After high school he moved to another part of New York City. In Greenwich Village he hoped to escape the poverty and racism of Harlem. A few years later he moved to Paris. He thought there he could live free from discrimination because of his color and sexual orientation. He lived in France for most of the rest of his life.

Baldwin published his first novel, *Go Tell It on the Mountain*, in 1953. The story is semi-autobiographical. It centers on the role of the Baptist church in the lives of the characters. Two years later he published *Notes of a Native Son.* This is a collection of powerful essays about his experiences with racism in the United States. One of Baldwin's most controversial novels, *Giovanni's Room*, was published in 1956. His publisher didn't want to publish it because the characters were white and gay. Many Americans at this time were hostile toward homosexuality. Baldwin's later books challenged the stereotypes of black men.

Baldwin's books published in the 1960s reflect the turmoil of the period. He periodically returned to the United States to write about the civil rights movement. He gave speeches, joined marches, participated in voter registration drives, and wrote articles for newspapers and magazines to support the cause of full legal rights for African Americans.

During the last decades of his life, Baldwin continued to write important works of fiction, nonfiction, and poetry. Over his forty-year career he wrote six novels, seven collections of essays, two plays, collections of poetry and short stories, a phototext, two dialogues, a screenplay, and a children's story. He became a powerful voice for victims of racism and homophobia.

CHAPTER 1

"I NEVER HAD A CHILDHOOD": HARLEM

T he men sitting on the stage at the Lincoln Memorial looked out over the National Mall. Hundreds of thousands of people, most of them black, stood listening. First one man, then another, spoke about rights and laws. The main speaker, Martin Luther King Jr., put aside his prepared remarks and spoke about dreams and equality and character. He electrified the crowd. Yet there was someone missing on that stage, another black man who also electrified crowds with words about equality. James Baldwin, whose book *The Fire Next Time* was a national best-seller and whose picture was on the cover of *Time* magazine, was in Washington, D.C., that day. Though considered a spokesman for his people, he was not invited to speak. He was a homosexual, a gay man before the word "gay" came in to common usage. Even worse for the crowd listening to speeches about human rights, he was a black gay man.

BORN INTO POVERTY

James Baldwin never knew his father. His mother, Emma Berdis Jones, was not married when she gave birth to James in Harlem, New York, on August 2, 1924. She soon married David Baldwin, a factory worker and part-time preacher. They took his last name. She delivered eight more children during the next fifteen years.

Life was difficult for the Baldwin family. Baldwin grew up during the Great Depression in a series of crowded tenement buildings in a poor, black ghetto. He had a difficult relationship with his stepfather. David was from the South. He had a fierce hatred for white people. He had witnessed the terrible discrimination of black people. He had seen beatings and lynchings. He ruled his family with rigid discipline. Baldwin was not allowed to play with his friends, see movies, or listen to the radio. "I never had a childhood," he told a reporter, according to Campbell.

Baldwin had two sources of comfort during this time. One source was his siblings, with whom he remained close during his entire life. In his book about his childhood, *The Fire Next Time*, Baldwin described the role his brothers and sisters played in his early life: "They kept me so busy caring for them, keeping them from the rats, roaches, falling plaster, and all the banality of poverty that I had no time to become a junkie or an alcoholic."

James Baldwin always felt a part of Harlem, the poor, black New York neighborhood in which he grew up.

Baldwin managed to care for his siblings while doing his favorite activity, reading. In the book, he wrote about his siblings, "As they were born, I took them over with one hand and held a book in the other." His two favorite books were *Uncle Tom's Cabin* by Harriet Beecher Stowe and Charles Dickens's *A Tale of Two Cities.* He also decided then that he wanted to be a writer. He was able to expand his passions when he entered school.

ENCOURAGED BY HIS TEACHERS

Because of his intelligence, Baldwin caught the attention of his teachers at Public School 24. Gertrude Ayer, one of the leading black educators in New York City, was the principal. She encouraged Baldwin to believe that poverty did not need to limit his horizons. The white drama teacher, Orilla Miller, also thought he was bright and talented. She took him to Broadway plays and put on his plays in her classroom. Baldwin wrote in *The Fire Next Time* that her actions were "my first key, my first clue that white people were human."

This belief in the kindness of white people was challenged when Baldwin was ten. While playing by himself in an empty lot, several white police officers called him racial slurs, then beat him. Experiences such as this were common for most black males of

One of Baldwin's favorite elementary school teachers was Harlem Renaissance poet Countee Cullen, who inspired Baldwin with stories of his travels to Paris.

the time. They became the basis for the anger and passion in his later writing.

Baldwin next attended Frederick Douglass Junior High School, named after the fearless abolitionist. It was considered an excellent school. One of the teachers who took an interest in Baldwin was Countee Cullen. He was one of the most celebrated poets of the Harlem Renaissance. He was the advisor to the school's literary club. He introduced his students to the works of Langston Hughes, Arna Bontemps, and other black writers of the time. Cullen had traveled widely. He inspired Baldwin with stories about Paris, France, worlds away from Harlem.

HARLEM RENAISSANCE

After World War I (1914–1918), Harlem became a cultural center for black artists, musicians, poets, writers, and dancers. Many migrated from the South to get away from the most oppressive forms of Jim Crow laws. In this upper Manhattan district they could more freely express their talents. W. E. B. DuBois was then the editor of *The Crisis*, the journal of the National Association for the Advancement of Colored People (NAACP). He published the art, stories, and poems of the period. Langston Hughes, Claude McKay, Zora Neale Hurston, and Baldwin's teacher Countee Cullen were among the poets and novelists who got their start during the Renaissance. The Cotton Club and the Apollo Theater attracted both black and white audiences. They came to listen to jazz and dance to the music of Duke Ellington and Eubie Blake.

The Harlem Renaissance did not do much to break down racial barriers among most residents. It did contribute to a burst of racial pride among black people. The arts movement significantly slowed with the stock market crash of 1929 and the Great Depression of the 1930s.

Baldwin was also encouraged by Herman Porter, a mathematics teacher who was advisor to the school newspaper, the *Douglass Pilot*. Porter provided a critical eye for the numerous stories, essays, and reviews that Baldwin submitted. Baldwin had read almost all of the books in the Harlem branch of the New York Public Library. Porter offered to take him to the main branch in the heart of midtown Manhattan. Baldwin was so nervous about entering white territory, he vomited on the bus. He soon became more comfortable there and began to visit often.

Baldwin had a harder time making friends with the students. He was small and not athletic. He had a large mouth and eyes, and he had been convinced by his stepfather that he was ugly. David had nicknamed his stepson Frog Eyes.

In his last year at Frederick Douglass, Baldwin was made editor-in-chief of the *Pilot*. Full of confidence from the encouragement of his teachers, he wrote about his ambition to become a playwright. During the summer before he went to high school, he experienced a profound religious event that heavily influenced his first published works.

A PROFOUND RELIGIOUS CONVERSION

Baldwin had been raised in churches where preachers moved congregations with powerful stories of

At age fourteen, James Baldwin became a preacher at a small, storefront church in Harlem.

heaven and hell, sin and redemption. Sometimes intense periods of music and preaching led church members to experience trances, visions, and fainting. These conversions led to even more commitment to their faith. When he was fourteen, Baldwin experienced a dramatic religious revelation in the church of a school friend. After listening to a dynamic minister named Mother Horn, he rose from his seat and fell to the floor. He was blinded by a vision he thought was from God. He began to train with Mother Horn to be a junior minister, preaching in neighborhood churches. The Harlem storefront churches became the backdrop for Baldwin's autobiographical account of a boy's religious conversion in *Go Tell It on the Mountain.*

A WHITE HIGH SCHOOL IN THE BRONX

Baldwin's teachers arranged for him to attend a prestigious high school in a white neighborhood, the Bronx. DeWitt Clinton High School had high standards. For a while, Baldwin struggled, earning poor grades in math and Spanish. However, he eagerly joined the *Magpie*, the school's literary magazine. He became lifelong friends with Emile Capouya and Richard Avedon, both of whom would later be part of the publishing world. Capouya introduced Baldwin to an older black friend, a painter who lived in Greenwich Village. Beauford Delaney in turn introduced Baldwin to the world of the arts, which thrived in the clubs and studios of the Village. Through Delaney Baldwin learned about the musicians Louis Armstrong and Ella Fitzgerald, writer Zora Neale Hurston, and other artists. This new world caused Baldwin to question his own world of the Pentecostal church. His doubts about his faith led Baldwin to leave the church and his preaching.

Baldwin graduated from high school in 1942, six months later than his schoolmates. His busy senior year left him behind on credits, and he needed to make them up. Major events were happening in both Baldwin's family and the world that year. His father's health was deteriorating, and he could no longer support his family. The United States had declared war on Japan and its allies, Germany and Italy. It was time for Baldwin to step up.

"I DID NOT KNOW WHO I WAS": GREENWICH VILLAGE

When James Baldwin graduated from high school in 1942, he was determined to be what he put in his school yearbook: novelist/playwright. Instead of going to college, however, he needed to support himself and his family. He first turned to work in Harlem, taking jobs such as elevator operator, dishwasher, and porter. He did not make much money. He knew that, with a war on, defense work would pay well and keep him out of the draft. Yet he would need to leave Harlem, where he had been protected from the harsh racism of the white world. With his friend Emile Capouya, he took a job in a defense factory in New Jersey.

Baldwin barely lasted a year there. The work was hard, but the labor wasn't his biggest difficulty. New Jersey followed Southern-style Jim Crow laws. Businesses were strictly segregated. Black residents were second-class citizens. Black workers were constantly persecuted by white bosses and coworkers. Baldwin tried to tolerate degrading slurs and bigoted insults. He was angered when he was turned away from restaurants and bowling alleys. He let out his frustrations at work, where he refused to act in a subservient way to white workers. Eventually, he was fired.

BACK TO HARLEM

Baldwin decided to return to Harlem. Before leaving, he and a friend went to a movie and then dinner at a segregated restaurant. As usual, the white waitress turned him away. Instead of leaving, Baldwin snapped. He picked up a water jug and hurled it at the waitress. It missed and shattered the mirror behind her. Baldwin managed to escape before police arrived. That was the first and last time he turned to violence to express his rage against racial prejudice and discrimination. From then on, he would use his words.

Baldwin could not escape violence during the racially tense period of the 1940s. Race riots had rocked Detroit, Michigan, in June 1943. Black residents were frustrated with poverty and poor treatment. Triggered by a rumor of the killing of a black serviceman by a white policeman, a riot broke out in the streets of Harlem a month later. Mobs of angry black residents looted and burned stores and other businesses. Baldwin's father had died a few days earlier, the same day his last child was born. David Baldwin's funeral was on the day

Baldwin witnessed a violent race riot in Harlem during the summer of 1943, when frustrated residents caused millions of dollars of damage to stores and businesses.

of the riot, coincidently James Baldwin's nineteenth birthday. Baldwin needed to escape the desperate conditions in Harlem. He needed to stay close, though, to support his mother and siblings. With the help of his friend Beaufort Delaney, he moved to Greenwich Village.

A NEW START IN GREENWICH VILLAGE

Baldwin lived a double life in his new surroundings. By day he worked odd jobs, whatever he could get to provide for his struggling family. By night he wrote the pages that would become his first novel, *Go Tell It on the Mountain.* He also threw himself into the nightlife of the Village. He frequented the bars and restaurants where writers, artists, and musicians socialized. One of the writers he idolized was Richard Wright, whose book *Native Son* had a profound effect on him. It was the story of a black man who accidently kills a white girl. The novel brought the devastating effects of bigotry and racism to the attention of white America. It became a huge bestseller.

Baldwin finally received a bit of luck. Through the efforts of a mutual friend, he arranged to meet Wright to show him some of his novel. Wright was impressed with the autobiographical story and thought that Baldwin had talent. Wright gave the pages to his publishers, Harper & Brothers. He also recommended Baldwin for the Eugene F. Saxon Foundation Fellowship, a grant for developing writers. Baldwin was awarded $500. He gave some of the money to his mother. He then settled down to finish the novel. He also needed a job. He found one

Richard Wright, already the author of a best-selling novel, encouraged Baldwin to finish his first book.

he liked, working as a waiter at a lively Village café. There he met celebrities, both black and white, such as Malcolm X, Henry Miller, Raul Robeson, Burt Lancaster, Eartha Kitt, and Marlon Brando, who became Baldwin's friend.

Despite the stimulating environment, this was one of Baldwin's most difficult periods. The Village was mostly white, and he had problems finding an apartment. He would ask a white friend to sign a lease

Actor Marlon Brando shared with Baldwin a passion for civil rights and remained a friend for Baldwin's entire life.

for him. Then, when the landlord discovered it was a black man who moved in, Baldwin would be evicted.

Baldwin was struggling with his sexuality during a time when homosexuality was both a legal and moral crime. It was also considered a mental illness. He had affairs with both men and women, including a long engagement with a female friend of Capouya's. Coping with the hostility of his immediate world while trying to work on his novel was exhausting. Being black in a white neighborhood was hard enough. "But the queer—not yet gay—world was an even more

EMPLOYMENT DISCRIMINATION FOR LESBIAN, GAY, BISEXUAL, TRANSGENDER, AND QUESTIONING (LGBTQ) WORKERS

James Baldwin's choice to openly live as a gay man was courageous. Because of persecution, homosexuals stayed in the closet until after World War II (1939–1945). The war brought people to large cities for work. There, homosexuals found community with each other without the disapproval of their families. Soon after the war, however, the Cold War (1947–1991) brought the fear of subversion. President Dwight D. Eisenhower became convinced that homosexuals were a danger to our country. He and Federal Bureau of Investigation (FBI) Director J. Edgar Hoover worried that they could be blackmailed into committing crimes such as spying for our enemies. This "Lavender Scare" resulted in Executive Order 10450, signed by Eisenhower in 1953. Homosexuals were to be hunted down and fired from government work.

Today, employment discrimination is the most common form of persecution of LGBTQ people in the United States. President Bill Clinton ended the 1953 policy in 1995. However, in 2014, it was legal to fire LBGTQ people in twenty-nine states.

intimidating area of this hall of mirrors. I knew that I was in the hall and present at this company—but the mirrors threw back only brief and distorted fragments of myself," Baldwin wrote later in *The Price of the Ticket*. Though often called insulting terms, he came out to new acquaintances as homosexual.

SUCCESS WRITING ARTICLES

Baldwin finished his novel, but no publishing house thought it ready to be published. He decided to work on smaller articles and reviews. Here, he started achieving successes. His insightful book reviews were published in prestigious journals such as the *Nation*. In 1947, the editors of a Jewish journal asked him to write an essay about the strained relationship between Jews and blacks. His essay, "The Harlem Ghetto," was published in *Commentary* in 1948. In this article, Baldwin points out that blacks were prejudiced against Jews in a similar way that whites were prejudiced against blacks. Prejudice had become part of our national tradition. This thoughtful analysis of race and religion earned Baldwin a national reputation. Other journals and magazines began asking for more articles and reviews.

Through his own hard work, James Baldwin had successfully transitioned from high school student to published writer. Yet his dream of being a novelist was not fulfilled. He didn't think he could write while battling the outside discrimination that came from being black and homosexual and the inside rage that overwhelmed him. "I didn't know who I was," he wrote one of his editors, according to Campbell. He decided to move to a place that many American writers had found welcoming. In 1948, using the money from a second writing grant, Baldwin bought a plane ticket and took off for France. He was moving to Paris.

CHAPTER 3

"THE WORLD IS BEFORE YOU": PARIS

When James Baldwin arrived in Paris on a chilly November day in 1948, he did not speak French. He had no job. He had only $40 in his pocket. But like American writers F. Scott Fitzgerald, Ernest Hemingway, and his mentor Richard Wright, he was hopeful that Paris would provide the peace he needed to finish his book. Campbell quotes a telling statement from an interview with Wright in a 1953 issue of *Ebony* magazine: "Every Negro in America carries all through his life the burden of race consciousness like a corpse on his back. I shed that corpse when I stepped off the train in Paris." Baldwin hoped to find the same freedom.

Baldwin was still haunted by an event that happened just two years earlier. He had a New York friend, a black man full of despair over the hard conditions of segregated America. The friend jumped to his death off the George Washington Bridge into the Hudson River. Baldwin recognized that many black Americans were becoming poisoned by the way they were treated

THE WORLD OF JIM CROW

James Baldwin's parents left the South for new opportunities in Northern states. They hoped to leave the oppressive practices of Jim Crow behind. These written and unwritten laws kept black people poor, segregated, and subservient. They were named after a character in a song that stereotyped black men. The laws governed behavior toward white people. There were numerous rules that black people had to follow. For instance, black people had to look down instead of making eye contact if passing white people on a sidewalk. Blacks had to address white people formally as "Mr. Smith" or "Sir." Whites addressed black people with their first name, or just "boy."

Businesses, churches, transportation, public facilities, and schools were completely segregated. In some states, textbooks for black children had to be stored in different warehouses than those for white children. Miscegenation laws made marriage between people of different races a felony punishable by many years in prison. If law enforcement agencies were too slow to impose penalties for breaking the rules, the Ku Klux Klan would take matters into its own hands.

White migrants to the North brought Jim Crow attitudes with them. There was no escape for black Americans unless, like James Baldwin and thousands of other blacks, they left the country.

Strict Jim Crow laws in the South created segregated schools, restaurants, and public facilities, such as restrooms.

by white Americans. He worried that his hatred would also cause him to self-destruct. Later Baldwin would realize that love was the antidote to the poison and the solution to racial problems. However, in 1948, Baldwin could only flee his country to save himself.

A DIFFICULT START IN PARIS

Paris was still suffering from the effects of the Nazi occupation during World War II. Buildings were damaged. Food and gasoline were still rationed. Jobs, especially for Americans, were scarce. Baldwin lived in a series of cheap hotels, trying to make his money last. At one point, he ended up in a French jail. Baldwin had complained to a fellow American writer that the sheets in his hotel were rarely changed. His friend provided a stolen sheet from another hotel. The chambermaid saw the sheet on Baldwin's bed and called the police.

The charges were eventually dropped, but Baldwin learned a bitter lesson. Prejudice toward those people perceived to be at the bottom of society was everywhere. When Baldwin came back to his hotel room after his court hearing, he attempted suicide. He tied the bed sheet around his neck and, standing on a chair, tied it to a ceiling pipe. When he kicked the chair away, the pipe broke, drenching the room with water. Baldwin left the hotel, renewing his dedication to life and his writing.

In Paris, Baldwin attempted to find his voice as a writer. In doing so he lost the friendship of Richard Wright. Baldwin wrote an article, "Everybody's Protest Novel," for a new magazine called *Zero*. In it he criticized novelists who used their stories for social protest. He attacked *Uncle Tom's Cabin*, which he had loved as a child. He also called *Native Son*, Wright's famous first novel, a failure. Wright was furious and ended their friendship. Baldwin never admitted it, but many critics think this attack was a way of setting himself apart from Wright. He was trying to establish a literary identity for himself. It worked. Editors from other publications soon requested articles for their magazines.

WRITING A NEW NOVEL

The next few years were productive ones for Baldwin. He fell in love with a handsome seventeen-year-old streetwise Swiss boy, Lucien Happersberger, who became the inspiration for his second novel, *Giovanni's Room*. When Baldwin complained that he couldn't write in Paris, Happersberger offered his parents' chalet in an isolated village in Switzerland. He tricked his parents into letting him use the house by sending them a set of stolen X-rays. They showed the beginnings of tuberculosis, a lung disease. He told his parents he needed to rest at the chalet and recover. The villagers had never seen a black man

Baldwin was only twenty-four when he moved to Paris to begin a new life free of the racial bigotry he found in the United States.

before. They would come up to Baldwin to touch his skin to see if the color would rub off. Left with just a typewriter and a couple of jazz records, Baldwin was able to finish his novel.

The book was finally titled *Go Tell It on the Mountain*, a reference to a black spiritual song. The autobiographical novel recounts the fourteenth birthday of a black youth, called John Grimes, in Harlem. There are three main conflicts: a young boy coming of age, clashes between father and son, and the boy's crisis of faith. Baldwin also brings in issues of racism and sexual identity. The novel gives readers insight into the devastating effects of bigotry and intolerance on black communities.

In 1952, Baldwin sent the book to his agent in New York, who found a publisher, Alfred A. Knopf. The editors wanted to meet with Baldwin to discuss revisions. Baldwin had no money to travel. Borrowing money from his friend Marlon Brando, he returned to New York. There, he was reminded of why he left in the first place. America in the 1950s was just as segregated as ever, though the civil rights movement was evolving. Baldwin's younger brother Wilmer had joined the newly desegregated U.S. Army, hoping to move up the ranks. However, he was harassed by racist officers. Baldwin warned Wilmer about falling into a trap of hatred, as he had. With a $1,000 advance from his publisher, Baldwin returned to Paris to work on his revisions.

Go Tell It on the Mountain was published in 1953. It received excellent reviews from the critics. They called it beautiful, fierce, masterful, poetic, and true. Encouraged, Baldwin went to work on new

Until 1948, black Americans who joined the military lived in segregated units, subject to inferior equipment and accommodations.

writing projects. "The world is before you," Campbell quotes from an editor's letter to Baldwin.

In Baldwin's absence, Happersberger had become involved with a young woman who became pregnant. Baldwin, though disappointed, encouraged Happersberger to marry her. Baldwin put his energy into writing a new work, this time a play. *The Amen Corner* was also based on his boyhood experiences with the Pentecostal church in Harlem. It received good reviews. In 1955, Baldwin returned to the United States to see it performed by the Howard University theater department. He was awarded a major grant by the prestigious Guggenheim Foundation. This was recognition that he was an important writer. He finally felt that he was a success.

CHAPTER 4

"MY AGENT TOLD ME TO BURN IT": SUCCESS

Baldwin's publisher wanted another novel. Again Baldwin isolated himself to write. This time he chose to live in a village in the south of France. This new novel was very different from his first. He decided to make his main characters white instead of black. One reason was that he did not want to be labeled as just a "Negro novelist." Creating white characters allowed Baldwin to put distance between himself and his story. He put himself in the skin of privileged white men. The themes of the book would still be autobiographical. Instead of struggling with racism, his main characters would struggle with homosexuality.

GIOVANNI'S ROOM

Giovanni's Room takes place in Paris. David, a young American, has fled his country as a way of denying his sexuality. He quickly meets and proposes marriage to a lively young American woman named Hella. She takes a trip to Spain to consider the proposal. While waiting for her answer, David becomes attracted to Giovanni, a young Italian bartender. However, Giovanni is already involved with his boss, Guillaume. Despite this, David and Giovanni fall in love. After many complications, Guillaume is found murdered in his bedroom. Giovanni is arrested for the crime, convicted, and sentenced to be executed. Hella finds out about the affair and David's homosexuality. She leaves him, returning to America. David is left alone in Paris in despair.

One of the major themes of the book is that homosexual love is not different from heterosexual love. Honest love cannot happen between two people unless they are honest with themselves. David denies his sexual identity, which prevents him from fully giving himself to any partner.

Baldwin was taking a huge risk in writing about this subject. Homosexuality was not as taboo in Paris as it was in America. In the United States, open homosexuals were persecuted and harassed by police. Even more common was discrimination in employment. People who were known to be homosexual were fired from their jobs. They became ostracized from their families and communities.

Baldwin was openly gay, but he kept his sexual life private. He didn't write a lot about it. When

Police raids on the Stonewall Inn, a gay bar in the Greenwich Village neighborhood of New York City, caused violent demonstrations by members of the gay community.

he did, it was in fiction. Baldwin appeared on talk shows when television became widespread. However, he was always a black spokesman, not a gay one. One of the very few essays in which he discussed homosexuality was "Preservation of Innocence." It was published in a 1949 issue of *Zero* and included in his 1998 *Collected Essays*. Many people thought that homosexuality was "unnatural." Baldwin wrote that it is "a phenomenon as old as mankind." He argued that people are too complex to put in any category, such as black, white, slave, free, male, female, straight, or gay. Baldwin resisted any categorization. "A novel insistently demands the presence and passion of human beings," he wrote, "who cannot ever be labeled."

A GAY LITERARY REVOLUTION

James Baldwin wrote at a time when it was risky to identify oneself as a homosexual. However, he was not the only writer to rise to fame as a gay author during the homophobic post-World War II time period. Other writers, mostly white, also courageously contributed books, poems, and plays that paved the way for a gay literary revolution.

Teens might be familiar with stories by gay authors through the films made of their books. Many movie fans will claim *Breakfast at Tiffany's* as one of their favorite films. The movie was based on a story by gay writer Truman Capote. His first novel, *Other Voices, Other Rooms*, is about a teenage boy's acceptance of his homosexuality. Other popular films that come from stories by a gay author include *Cabaret* and *A Single Man*. These were written by Christopher Isherwood, originally born in England but who became an American citizen in 1946. Another novelist who was a contemporary of Baldwin's is Gore Vidal. His novel *The City and the Pillar* showed its homosexual character as an athletic, masculine young man.

Though they are not always identified as gay, homosexual playwrights and poets are often found in high school English textbooks. The plays *The Glass Menagerie*, *Cat on a Hot Tin Roof*, and *A Streetcar Named Desire* were written by gay playwright Tennessee Williams during the 1940s and '50s. Students may read poems by Allen Ginsberg, a pioneer of the Beat movement in the 1950s. Ginsberg was a gay man as well.

GAY PERSECUTION

In 1955, Baldwin took *Giovanni's Room* to the United States. "My agent told me to burn it," said Baldwin, according to biographer Lisa Rosset. His agent was afraid he would alienate both his black and his white readers. His editors at Knopf refused to publish it. They were worried that they might be prosecuted for obscenity. The 1950s were a hostile period for those considered "deviant." Wisconsin

Senator Joe McCarthy's anticommunist crusade also targeted homosexuals. Gays were being scapegoated and asked to resign from government jobs. Despite *Giovanni's Room*'s subject matter, another publisher, Dial Press, agreed to publish the novel. It came out in 1956 with a dedication to his friend Lucien Happersberger.

The reviews were mostly favorable. Baldwin biographer David Leeming recorded some of the reviews. One critic called Baldwin one of the best young writers to come on the scene in a long time. The *New York Times* reviewer said that Baldwin had handled a sensitive subject with "dignity and intensity." Another reviewer said it was "beautifully written" and "nearly heroic." There were also criticisms of the subject matter of the book. Black readers wanted Baldwin to establish himself as the spokesperson for their rights, instead of writing about gay, white characters. His gay audience was upset that the openly gay character, Giovanni, dies a horrible death at the end of the book. The character who is ashamed of his homosexuality goes on living. Baldwin, says Leeming, had only one answer to the criticism. *Giovanni's Room* is "not about homosexual love. It's what happens to you if you are afraid to love anybody."

Like his characters, Baldwin struggled with love. Happersberger remained friends with him, but they did not have the relationship Baldwin would have liked.

His newfound success allowed him to travel wherever he wanted. He had many friends, but a series of meaningless affairs left him even lonelier. He wrote in his book *Nobody Knows My Name,* "There are few things on earth more futile or more deadening than a meaningless round of conquests." He questioned whether he should remain in Europe.

SUCCESS AS A WRITER

While Baldwin was waiting for *Giovanni's Room* to be published, he put together a collection of his previously published essays. He called it *Notes of a Native Son.* It was both a tribute to Wright's novel and a recognition that he, too, was a son of the American society. Though the civil rights movement was heating up, Baldwin's message was one of tolerance and integration. In one essay, "Ruminations Upon the Death of a Father," he describes his personal belief: "One must

never, in one's own life accept…injustices as common-
place, but must fight them with all one's strength. This
fight begins, however, in the heart." Acceptance of
oneself is a theme in many of his books.

In his essays, Baldwin
attacks both black and
white stereotypes of
African Americans, and
recounts how experiences
of racism affected him.

Notes of a Native Son is a good introduction to Baldwin as an essayist. It contains pieces about growing up in Harlem and life in Paris. It has Baldwin's opinions on racial issues. Poet Langston Hughes reviewed the book for the *New York Times.* According to Campbell, Hughes said that Baldwin was some way off from being "a great artist in writing." He was too obsessed with race. If he could "look at life purely as himself and for himself," Hughes wrote, "America and the world might well have a major contemporary commentator." Hughes's prediction was prophetic.

Others in the literary world thought that Baldwin already had earned his accolades. In 1956, he was awarded a fellowship by the *Partisan Review*, a prestigious literary magazine.

Baldwin sometimes found it difficult to balance his love for social occasions with his need to isolate himself to write.

He also received the National Institute of Arts and Letters Award. It praised him for the combination of objectivity and passion with which he approached his subject matter. At age thirty-two, Baldwin had become an accomplished writer with an international readership.

Despite being open about his homosexuality, Baldwin was popular in many social circles, both black and white. His friend Peter Daily describes him this way: "'Jimmy' (as he soon became even to casual acquaintances) was an urbane man with sophisticated manners...[he] was elegant, humorous, and playful." He rose late in the morning and met friends all afternoon and evening. He then stayed up late in the night to write. Daily witnessed days where "the flow of conversation rarely flagged, animated by his apparently inexhaustible fund of exuberance and high spirits. Before we knew it, afternoon would lengthen into evening, bringing with it the uneasy sense of missed appointments or work neglected." There were events, however, which would bring these high spirits down close to despair.

Baldwin was attending an international conference of black writers and artists in Paris in the fall of 1956. In America, the civil rights movement was gaining momentum. Baldwin tried to keep up with developments, but he felt distanced from the struggle. During a lunch break, he went out to get

Fifteen-year-old Dorothy Counts faced fierce racial prejudice when she became the first black student to attend Harding High School in Charlotte, North Carolina, in 1957.

a newspaper. There on the front page was a photo-graph of Dorothy Counts. She was a fifteen-year-old black high school girl in Charlotte, North Carolina. She was walking into her school while white students spat at her and shouted insults. Baldwin wrote about the incident in his book about the civil rights era, *No Name in the Street.* It "made me furious, it filled me with both hatred and pity, and it made me ashamed...I could no longer sit around in Paris." He decided it was time to go home.

CHAPTER 5

"A BITTERLY HOSTILE COUNTRY": THE CIVIL RIGHTS MOVEMENT

James Baldwin arrived home in 1957 to a country very much different from the one he left ten years earlier. In 1947, the year before he left for Paris, black baseball player Jackie Robinson put on a Brooklyn Dodgers uniform and played in his first Major League game. A year later, President Harry Truman ended segregation in the military. The 1950s would bring even more changes.

The United States was asserting its leadership in the world after World War II. Many allied nations, however, put pressure on it to begin resolving its racial issues. How could a country promote freedom against communism around the world when so many of its people were second-class citizens? This was one reason why the Supreme Court in 1954 ruled against school segregation in *Brown v. Board of Education*. Black leaders such as A. Philip Randolph and Bayard Rustin rallied black citizens for change. They demanded greater rights and equal protection under the law. If segregation had no place in America's schools, perhaps it had no place anywhere.

CIVIL RIGHTS CHALLENGES

One of the first victories of the civil rights movement toward integration took place in Montgomery, Alabama, in 1955. Led by Rosa Parks, Martin Luther King Jr., Jo Ann Robinson, and Ralph Abernathy, fifty thousand working men and women boycotted segregated city buses. After more than a year, the Supreme

African Americans walked to work instead of riding the bus during the Montgomery, Alabama, bus boycott in 1956.

Court ruled that Montgomery's bus laws were unconstitutional. This success led to more nonviolent challenges to segregation in the South.

Racist whites did not stand by peacefully. The Ku Klux Klan and White Citizens' Councils reacted with firebombs, lynchings, and other forms of violence. A new elementary school in Nashville, Tennessee, was dynamited after registering its first black child. Rioting occurred after a black student had been admitted to the University of Alabama. The governor of Arkansas sent in the state militia to prevent black students from entering Little Rock's Central High School.

BALDWIN SEES FOR HIMSELF

Baldwin was determined to see for himself the civil rights battles in the South. He was particularly impressed with the courage of schoolchildren who were at the front line of desegregation. He obtained an assignment for an article from *Harper's* magazine and set off for Charlotte, North Carolina. He had never been to the South before, though both his parents had left the South to find new opportunities in the North. In *No Name in the Street* he describes it as "territory absolutely hostile and exceedingly strange." In Charlotte, three years after the *Brown* decision, only four children had been able to register for newly desegregated schools. Only three managed to attend. The fourth student, Dorothy Counts, was spat on and harassed so much while trying to attend the all-white high school that she gave up.

Baldwin next traveled to Atlanta, Georgia. There, he experienced Jim Crow firsthand. He was forced to

After meeting Martin Luther King Jr. in 1957, Baldwin became inspired to write about civil rights in the United States.

sit at the back of a segregated city bus. He arranged to meet Martin Luther King Jr., who was in Atlanta visiting his parents. King, a pastor at a Baptist church in Montgomery, Alabama, had emerged as

the leader of the civil rights struggle in the South. Baldwin was impressed with King's dedication to the nonviolent teachings of Mahatma Gandhi in India. Baldwin found that he and King shared a belief that hatred must be replaced by love. King predicted that the determination and solidarity among blacks in the South would soon end segregation. Baldwin thought the process would be long and violent.

Baldwin followed King back to Montgomery to hear him preach. The sermon was unlike anything he had ever heard in a church. King called on his congregation to work together to overcome the crime, poverty, and poor education forced on them by the white community. He

urged them to take responsibility for their own freedom. He did not mention that his house had recently
been firebombed.

A LETTER FROM HARLEM

Baldwin returned to New York ready to write his
articles. He was deeply moved by the dedication to
the movement and fearlessness of the people who
defied segregation in the South. As Campbell put it,
"As much as it was a magazine assignment, this first
journey to the South was a voyage of discovery and
rite of initiation." He was convinced that he had a
duty to make all Americans aware of the struggle for
civil rights. Baldwin's articles were very well received.
Readers began to look to him as the spokesman for
the civil rights movement.

In 1960, Baldwin returned to Harlem. He was
shocked at its deterioration. His old neighborhood
was called "Junkie's Hollow" because of all the
drug dealing. His old tenement was replaced by a
low-rent, high-rise apartment complex. Instead of
helping residents, Baldwin believed, the complexes
were bleak, characterless places that isolated people
from their culture and communities. In his *Esquire*
magazine article "Fifth Avenue Uptown: A Letter
from Harlem," later collected in *Nobody Knows My
Name*, he described the white police who patrolled

the streets. They were "like an occupying soldier in a bitterly hostile country."

Both black and white readers were outraged by the article. They demanded that Baldwin print a retraction. Baldwin was saddened by the reaction, but he refused to take back his criticisms. The South, he thought, was changing for the better. The Northern ghettos were getting worse. Baldwin returned to Paris but felt so drawn to the fight for rights in the United States that he began a regular shuttle between Paris and New York.

EVERYBODY KNOWS MY NAME

A collection of Baldwin's essays on civil rights was published in 1961. *Nobody Knows My Name* was a great success. Baldwin became the best-known and most important black writer in America. The book stayed on the nonfiction best-seller list for six months. The thirteen essays are wide ranging in topic. Most of them lead to Baldwin's main theme. He writes in the introduction, "The connection between American whites and blacks is far deeper and more passionate than any of us like to think." The races are tied together by history, blood, and the common interest in the future of the country.

Baldwin became more popular than ever. He was in demand for speaking engagements, interviews,

Instead of focusing on the differences between black and white Americans that divided them, Baldwin challenged his readers to consider the connections that united them.

and social events. Baldwin loved staying up all night and socializing with his thousands of friends, both old and new. He tried to keep his commitments to civil rights organizations. All this constant activity left little time to write. His publisher was asking for a new novel. Baldwin needed to find a quiet place to focus on the book he had been sporadically working on for six years. He found that place in Istanbul, Turkey.

ANOTHER COUNTRY DISAPPOINTS AND DAZZLES

Baldwin thought his new novel, *Another Country* (1962), was his best one so far. He worried, though, about the public reaction. Set in Greenwich Village in the 1950s, the story focuses on the last days of Rufus Scott, a black jazz drummer. His romantic relationship with Leona, a white woman from the South, is deteriorating. She suffers a serious breakdown, and Rufus commits suicide by jumping off the George Washington Bridge. Other characters include Rufus's sister Ida, a jazz singer; her lover Vivaldo, an actor; and Eric, who loves both Rufus and Vivaldo. Gay love, straight love, bisexual love, extramarital love, and interracial love are all mixed up in multiple plot lines that are not all resolved at the end. The characters, though, move away from fear and closer to the knowledge of self that leads to honest love.

JAMES BALDWIN AND THE FBI

The FBI put many civil rights activists under secret investigation during the 1950s and 1960s. During the early days of the Cold War, its job was to protect America from communist revolutionaries who worked to overthrow the government. James Baldwin came under the scrutiny of the FBI when he briefly joined a pro-Cuba organization. Cuba was a communist country allied with the Soviet Union. Baldwin complained to the FBI about harassment. He had reason to be concerned. Martin Luther King Jr. was also watched closely. The FBI wiretapped his phones, listened to his conversations, and collected information that could be used to blackmail him.

The FBI also protected Americans from obscenity. They confiscated books considered obscene according to strict laws during this time. A citizen in New Orleans, Louisiana, complained to the FBI when a local bookstore stocked copies of one of Baldwin's books. The FBI director, J. Edgar Hoover, took no action against the bookseller. He did, however, send the citizen publications titled "Combating Merchants of Filth: The Role of the FBI" and "The Fight Against Filth."

Another Country was controversial from the moment it was published. Some critics called it obscene, though the sex scenes are tame compared to other novels published at the time. Other critics called the writing sloppy, lifeless, and stilted. According to Campbell, the critic Stanley Edgar Hyman wrote in a review, "The writing is bad by any standard and exceptionally bad by Baldwin's own high standard." Campbell thought Baldwin had too many competing interests over the seven years of writing to write a disciplined, well-crafted long piece.

He wrote, "The compact, jeweled prose of *Go Tell It on the Mountain* here turns to paste."

The public loved the book. When it was reissued in paperback in 1963, it was the second-largest-selling book of the year. It brought Baldwin fame and fortune. It also brought him to the attention of the FBI. According to Campbell, FBI Director J. Edgar Hoover thought the novel and its author were "perverted." There were no federal laws broken, however. An FBI file was opened on Baldwin that eventually grew to 1,750 pages.

"THE FIRE NEXT TIME": SPOKESMAN

J ames Baldwin threw himself into civil rights work. Though he realized his best platform was through his writing, he also became involved in some of the important civil rights events of the 1960s. He developed relationships with important leaders, both black and white, who impacted the movement. He used time on buses and in airplanes to write novels, stories, articles, and another play. It was during the '60s that he was at the pinnacle of his influence.

A CHALLENGE TO NONVIOLENCE

Baldwin believed in the message of nonviolence practiced by Martin Luther King Jr. In 1960, he joined the Congress of Racial Equality (CORE), a civil rights organization based in the South. At that

Baldwin was a charismatic speaker who was often invited to speak to students on college campuses.

time CORE was organizing sit-ins to desegregate restaurants. He toured the South giving speeches to raise money for CORE and other civil rights organizations. Audiences found the former teen preacher inspirational and charismatic.

Not every black activist held views similar to King's and other mainstream leaders. Some thought that the pace of change was too slow. They believed that the movement called for more radical methods. Two of these were leaders in the Nation of Islam, Elijah Muhammad and Malcolm X. They were winning followers in the North. Black Muslims, as they were called, asked blacks to reject any tie with white society. They preached a message of economic self-sufficiency as opposed to integration with whites. They promoted self-defense instead of nonviolence. Their beliefs were based on traditional Islam instead of Christianity.

Although Baldwin did not like the Black Muslims' extremist views, in 1962 he accepted an invitation to meet with Elijah Muhammad in Chicago, Illinois. Muslim religious beliefs did not permit alcohol or tobacco. Muslims taught that homosexuality was evil. While Baldwin did not find much in common with the Black Muslims, he used this encounter as the basis for his essay "Letter from a Region in My Mind," later collected in his book *The Fire Next Time.*

THE FIRE NEXT TIME

In his essay, Baldwin warned America that the rising tide of black militancy is dangerous. He argued that the answer to the country's racial problems

James Baldwin and Bayard Rustin were shocked by the murder of four black children who were killed in a bombing of a church in Birmingham, Alabama, in 1963.

65

is not division but unity. He thinks that the Black Muslims' call for separation is just as racist as the whites' fight for segregation. The challenge, he wrote, is to create a society where "the value placed on the color of the skin is always and everywhere and forever a delusion." He ends his essay with this warning. "If we do not now dare everything, the fulfillment of that prophecy, re-created from the Bible in song by a slave, is upon us: God gave Noah the rainbow sign, No more water, the fire next time."

The book became a national bestseller. Baldwin was asked to make television and radio interviews. He won the George Polk Award for outstanding magazine journalism. He appeared on the cover of the May 17, 1963, issue of *Time* magazine. Many Americans thought that Baldwin was the top spokesman for the struggle for civil rights in America.

The leaders of the civil rights organizations were ambivalent about Baldwin's role. They were uneasy about his sexuality. They were worried that it could be used to discredit the movement. Homosexuality was a sin in their Baptist beliefs. Though Baldwin kept in contact with King during this time, he, like another homosexual activist, Bayard Rustin, was kept at a distance. Neither of the men, despite their huge commitment to the cause of civil rights, were invited to speak or even sit on the stage for King's famous "I Have a Dream" speech during the historic March on Washington.

RACIAL UNREST IN THE SOUTH

In 1963, Baldwin traveled to Jackson, Mississippi, to meet with Medgar Evers, the head of the Jackson chapter of the National Association for the Advancement of Colored People (NAACP). He also met with James Meredith. A year earlier, Meredith was the first black student to attend the University of Mississippi. Mobs of white students had rioted to keep him from entering the campus. President John F. Kennedy had to send federal troops to escort him to class.

THE MURDER OF EMMETT TILL

James Baldwin learned about the murder of Emmett Till during his visit to the South in 1963. In August 1955, fourteen-year-old Till arrived from Chicago for a visit with family in Money, Mississippi. He was unaware of the unwritten laws of the South called Jim Crow. On a dare, he flirted with a white woman in a grocery store. Three days later, he was dragged from his bed in the middle of the night. His killers beat him, shot him in the head, and threw him in the Tallahatchie River. His mutilated body was found three days later.

Mamie Till, Emmett's mother, insisted on an open-casket funeral. Tens of thousands of people were horrified to see Emmett's maimed and distorted face. A photo of his dead body was on the cover of national magazines.

Till's two white killers were identified by his uncle. They were arrested and went to trial for murder. An all-white jury acquitted them. The killers then bragged about the murder to a journalist. The failure of the federal government to do anything made national and international news. Among the shocked Southerners was a black woman named Rosa Parks. Three months after Till's murder, she refused to give up her seat on a Montgomery, Alabama, city bus. The civil rights movement had begun.

As a NAACP field worker, Evers had investigated the murder of Emmett Till in 1955. Now Baldwin accompanied Evers as he was investigating the murder of a black man by a white storekeeper. Baldwin took notes on their dangerous trek into the Mississippi backwoods looking for evidence. According to Rosset, Baldwin thought Evers "had the calm of somebody who knows he's going to die." Three months later, Evers was murdered by white racists in front of his wife and children.

Baldwin was shocked by the next series of events in the South, this time in Birmingham, Alabama. The governor of the state, George Wallace, pledged, "Segregation now! Segregation tomorrow! Segregation forever!" King issued the Birmingham Manifesto, demanding the integration of restaurants and restrooms. Schoolchildren organized into a Children's Crusade to march for desegregation. The American public was horrified

to see news footage of the Birmingham police force, led by Commissioner of Public Safety Bull Connor, brutally attacking the children with high-powered water hoses and vicious police dogs.

Hundreds of schoolchildren in Birmingham, Alabama, were arrested and sent to jail for marching to integrate restaurants and public facilities in 1963.

INSIDE THE HEART
OF PREJUDICE

U.S. Attorney General Robert Kennedy asked Baldwin to organize a meeting with black leaders to see what the federal government could do to end the violence. The meeting did not go well. Some participants became defensive and did not listen. However, within a few weeks President John F. Kennedy submitted a sweeping civil rights bill to Congress. While segregationists bitterly debated the bill, violence continued. Eighteen days after the March on Washington, four little black girls in Birmingham, Alabama, were killed when a bomb was thrown into their church.

During this time Baldwin finished his play, *Blues for Mr. Charlie.* He dedicated it to the four innocent black girls killed in Birmingham. Loosely based on Emmett Till's story, the main character, Richard Henry, is a young black jazz musician who returns to the South after living in New York for a few years. He becomes active in his town's civil rights activities. He angers a local store owner, Lyle, who kills him. An all-white jury acquits Lyle. The play opened on Broadway in 1964 to mixed reviews. Baldwin became bitter when his friend Lucien Happersberger met and married the female lead in the play, though the marriage barely lasted a year.

The mid-1960s were a pivotal time for Baldwin. More white people than black people were reading

his books. He was often in the company of prominent leaders and entertainers. For all his fame,
white cab drivers would still not pick him up. He
still had to have Happersberger as a front man to
rent an apartment for him in white neighborhoods.
He was devastated when President Kennedy was
assassinated in 1963 in Texas. In spite of the continued racial unrest, Baldwin was hopeful for the
future. He was ready to continue the fight for civil
rights any way he could.

CHAPTER 7

"SOMETHING HAS ALTERED IN ME": ASSASSINATIONS

n 1964, James Baldwin was restless. He continued to be actively involved in the civil rights movement. A new generation of younger, more violent, leaders was taking charge on the West Coast. Baldwin reached out to them, trying to understand their philosophy. Yet he was a writer, and he needed isolation to write. He bought a house in southern France, but returned to New York frequently. While there, he worked at a frantic pace speaking at conferences, writing articles, and giving interviews. In his writing, he continued to explore the issues that troubled him from the beginning of his writing career: identity, prejudice, and racism.

DEBATING AMERICA'S FUTURE

Baldwin traveled to England in 1965 to participate in a debate at Cambridge University. His opponent was William F. Buckley, the white editor of the *National Review*, a political journal. The topic was

"The American Dream and the American Negro." According to Baldwin biographer W. J. Weatherby, Buckley called Baldwin a "posturing hero" who received satisfaction by criticizing America. Baldwin responded, speaking for all black Americans: "I dammed a lot of rivers, I laid a lot of track, I hoed a lot of cotton, I cleaned a lot of dishes. You wouldn't have had this country if it hadn't been for me." Cambridge students overwhelming voted Baldwin the winner of the debate.

VIOLENCE CONTINUES

While Baldwin was in England, he heard that Malcolm X had been shot by members of the Nation of Islam. Malcolm had split with the church after a pilgrimage to Mecca. He had tempered his fiery speech against white people. He was willing to work with Dr. King. He and Baldwin had become friends after Malcolm showed up to one of Baldwin's lectures. Baldwin didn't necessarily agree with all of Malcolm's views. However, he respected the man. Baldwin wrote to change white prejudice and bigotry. Malcolm's targeted audience was the hearts and minds of oppressed black people.

Baldwin was devastated by the assassination. Newspaper reporters hounded him for his reaction. "That bullet was forged in the crucible of the West," Baldwin biographer Randall Kenan quotes from a

Though Baldwin did not agree with all of Malcolm X's beliefs, he was devastated when Malcolm was murdered in 1965.

London newspaper interview with Baldwin: "That death was dictated by the most successful conspiracy in the history of the world, and its name is white supremacy." Many readers thought these comments were more examples of Baldwin's growing extremism.

In March 1965, Baldwin participated in a march from Selma to Montgomery, Alabama, to support Martin Luther King Jr.'s push for voting rights. Seventy-two percent of the South's eligible voters had stayed home on Election Day rather than risk their lives. Alabama's black citizens were often threatened

Baldwin spoke to participants after a march from Selma to Montgomery, Alabama, in 1965 to support voting rights for African Americans in the South.

with violence when they tried to register to vote. The state had enacted many barriers to black registration, such as literacy tests and special voting taxes called poll taxes. Earlier in the month, the TV-watching nation had been interrupted by videos of police attacking protesting schoolchildren with cattle prods and clubs. King's push in Selma produced results. By August of that year, President Lyndon B. Johnson had signed a sweeping Voting Rights Act.

A NEW SPOKESMAN FOR CIVIL RIGHTS

Some of his readers thought that Baldwin was becoming too extreme. And then there were some who thought he was not extreme enough. Stokely Carmichael, the new young leader of the Student Nonviolent Coordinating Committee (SNCC), called for an overthrow of the existing political order. Despite his organization's title, he advocated using violence to establish a separate black society. Out West, in the black ghettos of Oakland, California, a group of radical activists were gaining publicity for promoting revolution. Led

by cofounder Eldridge Cleaver, the Black Panthers preached a message of "black power" to young black activists tired of the slow pace of the nonviolent movement. Instead of protest signs, they carried loaded guns.

The Black Panthers in California became impatient with Martin Luther King Jr.'s message of nonviolence and called for "Black Power."

Writing from prison, Cleaver published an essay about James Baldwin called "Notes on a Native Son" in the August 1966 issue of *Ramparts* magazine and then in his 1968 book, *Soul On Ice*. He accused Baldwin of hating himself and other black people. He called Baldwin's homosexuality a "sickness" and a "racial death wish." He wrote that Baldwin's books were a war on masculinity. According to Kenan, Baldwin responded, "All that toy soldier has done is call me gay." He supported the Black Panthers for their message of black pride. He continued to disagree with their violent methods.

THE STONEWALL RIOTS

As a neighborhood bar, the Stonewall Inn in Greenwich Village was a dive. Operated by the New York Mafia, it didn't have an alcohol license and it had no running water. Yet gay patrons could put a quarter in the jukebox and dance with each other, a crime in New York and most other places. Like other gay bars, it was regularly raided by police. They would turn on lights, check identifications, arrest those in drag, and tell everyone else to go home. In the 1960s, the police began putting more pressure on New York's gay community, arresting over one hundred gay citizens each week. This produced a lot of anger and tension, especially for those fearful of discovery.

Early in the morning of June 28, 1969, New York police raided the Stonewall Inn. Instead of following the usual pattern, the bar patrons refused to cooperate. The police decided to arrest everyone. However, the patrol wagons took a long time to arrive. A crowd assembled outside. Some began throwing cans and bottles at the police, who called for reinforcements. The police eventually cleared the street in front of the bar. Over the next six days the crowds and police battled each other. The widespread publicity brought by events at Stonewall made it the birthplace of gay liberation.

Baldwin kept writing, but he was finding that his books were less well received than in the past. In 1968, he published his novel *Tell Me How Long the Train's Been Gone.* This is the story of Leo Proudhammer, a successful black bisexual actor from a poor background. He works hard to escape the Harlem ghetto, but he can't find his place in white society. He struggles with living in the spotlight of fame. He is also confused by his sexuality. All of these themes mirrored Baldwin's own personal issues.

Columbia Pictures asked Baldwin to write a screenplay about the life of Malcolm X. He eventually abandoned the project when the studio asked for too many revisions.

THE DREAM IS GONE

When Martin Luther King Jr. was assassinated in April 1968 by a racist white man, Baldwin was devastated. He wrote in *No Name in the Street* that something died in him, "…something has altered in me, something has gone away." His grief and frustration were obvious to everyone around him. The same rage against prejudice and bigotry caused blacks to riot in major cities. Baldwin attended King's funeral, then made plans to leave the country. Full of bitterness and despair, he would never again make America his home.

CHAPTER 8

"HIS VOICE, HIS STRENGTH, AND HIS CROWN": LEGACY

The months following Martin Luther King Jr.'s death were dark ones for Baldwin. He traveled from New York, to London, to Italy and Istanbul, and to Paris. He told Weatherby, "I didn't think I could write at all, I didn't see any point to it.... I didn't know how to continue, didn't see my way clear." He looked noticeably older and seemed ill and frail. Grief, exhaustion, and late-night socializing brought on hospitalizations to rest and recuperate. In 1970, he bought a house in the south of France where family and friends could visit. He still followed events in the United States and contributed his support to causes he thought worthwhile.

WRITING AGAIN

Baldwin did begin writing again. He continued with his same themes: how identity is shaped by prejudice and the destruction caused by bigotry. In 1972, he published *No Name in the Street*, an

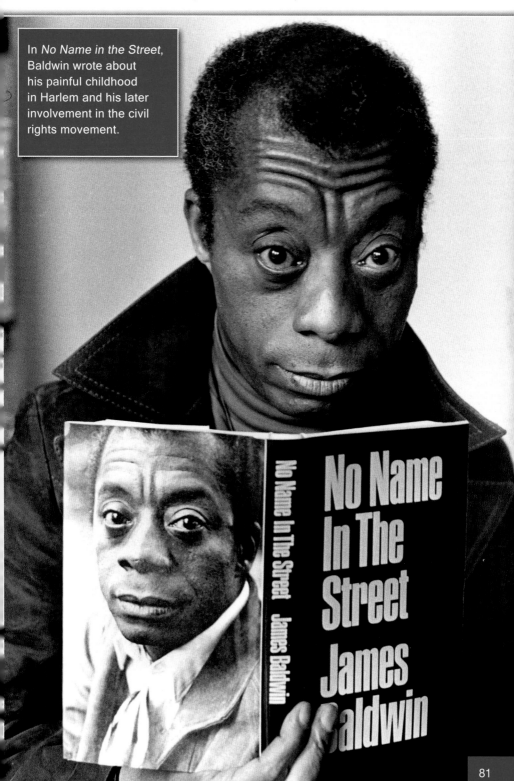

In *No Name in the Street*, Baldwin wrote about his painful childhood in Harlem and his later involvement in the civil rights movement.

autobiographical account of his civil rights activities. It is angrier and more bitter than his previous books. He tries to explain the frustration and desperation that led to race riots in Los Angeles, California; Washington, D.C.; New York City; Chicago; Pittsburgh, Pennsylvania; and other American cities. He rails against the U.S. government, which he says allies itself with racist whites. He predicts new waves of violence.

Baldwin's next novel, *If Beale Street Could Talk*, continues with the same tone. He narrates the story through a female character. Nineteen-year-old Tish is a black, pregnant shop assistant in Harlem. Her boyfriend, Fonny, is in jail on a false charge of rape. Baldwin uses the story to attack the American judicial system, which he believed targeted and destroyed young black men. Like most of his later works, the book received mixed reviews, though it spent many weeks on the best-seller lists.

PROFESSOR BALDWIN

Baldwin's fame and prestige brought him an offer to teach college students. He called it his second career. In 1978, he was invited to teach courses in American literature and creative writing at Bowling Green State University in Ohio. In 1983, he accepted a position at a network of five colleges in Massachusetts. Baldwin found that he enjoyed lively debates and discussions with students, though sometimes his lectures were composed on the fly. He wanted students to learn the history of civil rights through his own experiences. He was also popular with faculty, hosting parties late into the night. His teaching was soon curtailed by poor health. The constant traveling back and forth to Europe and his habits of chain smoking and drinking were catching up with him. In 1983, he was hospitalized with a mild heart attack.

DISAPPOINTMENT AND RECOGNITION

Baldwin's last works did not bring him the attention that his earliest books did. He believed that he was still writing with the same skill and power as ever, but the critics did not want to hear his message. In 1979, he published the novel *Just Above My Head*, which he dedicated to his brothers and sisters. It is a long book full of preachers, jazz, homosexual love, and black pride. Like his other novels, the theme speaks about the redeeming power of love. Critics thought that the book badly needed revision to tighten up the focus.

Just Above My Head became controversial because it was largely written in Black English, a vernacular Baldwin grew up speaking. During this time educators debated the use of Black English among students. Some educators thought Black English should be discouraged in favor of standard English. Baldwin wrote in a *New York Times* article that among African Americans, Black English is "a political instrument" and "the most crucial key to identity." He argued that Black English is just as legitimate a language as any other.

Baldwin also received the kind of attention that he did not want. After so many assassinations in the 1960s of prominent black leaders, he sometimes feared for his life. A threatening incident in 1980 showed that he may have had something to fear. He and Nigerian writer Chinua Achebe were holding a public discussion at the University of Florida. Halfway through, a shortwave radio operator's voice came crackling over his microphone. According to Campbell, Baldwin tried to ignore it. But soon the words were loud and clear. "You gonna have to cut it out, Mr. Baldwin. We can't stand

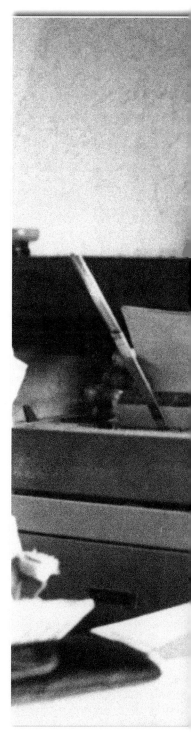

At the end of his life, Baldwin returned to his home in southern France. He was surrounded by family and friends during his final days.

for this kind of going on." Baldwin was shocked, but responded, "If you assassinate me in the next two minutes, I'm telling you this: it no longer matters what you think. The doctrine of white supremacy on which the Western world is based has had its hour, has had its day—it's over!" Baldwin did not call the police. He thought the intimidators might have been the police themselves.

In 1985, Baldwin finished what would become his last book, *The Evidence of Things Not Seen*. It had started out as an article for *Playboy* magazine about a series of child murders in Atlanta, Georgia. Twenty-eight black children had been murdered between 1979 and 1982. Police could link the black man accused of the crimes to only two of the deaths. Many people thought that the police would have worked harder to find other possible suspects if the children were white. Baldwin used the book to show that race relations in the South were still troubled.

THE FINAL DAYS

Baldwin was recognized with many awards in the last decade of his life. He received honorary degrees from Morehouse College in Atlanta in 1976, the University of Massachusetts in 1978, and the City University of New York in 1982. In 1986, he received France's highest award, the Legion of Honor, for bringing honor to the country.

CENSORSHIP OF LGBTQ MATERIALS IN SCHOOL LIBRARIES

Can you find *Giovianni's Room* in your school library? Does the library include books with LGBTQ characters and themes? Many gay and straight students find that they feel more supported when their libraries are inclusive. This means the libraries contain resources about diverse people and lifestyles. Most school librarians buy fiction and nonfiction books and subscribe to online services that help teens find information about LGBTQ people, history, and events. The 2011 National School Climate Survey found that LGBTQ students in schools with these resources get better grades, have fewer absences, and have fewer experiences of harassment and assault.

In some school districts, parents have attempted to remove materials they find offensive to their beliefs. For instance, in 2012, a Utah parent requested the removal of a children's book that featured a lesbian couple with a family. She thought it made a lifestyle she didn't agree with look normal. High school students at Governor Mifflin Senior High School in Pennsylvania in 2012 found that LGBTQ websites were blocked on school computers, but sites for organizations that condemn homosexuality were not.

The U.S. Supreme Court has ruled that schools may not remove books from school libraries because they don't like the books' politics. Students can request that libraries buy LBGTQ-themed books that are recommended by the American Library Association or the National Coalition Against Censorship. They can also ask permission to present a display in the library during Pride month.

In 1987, Baldwin stopped teaching and returned to his home in France. He had a painful sore throat and felt ill. A doctor diagnosed cancer of the esophagus. Surgery did not help stop the disease. Baldwin died at his home in southern France with family and friends at his side. Five thousand people attended his funeral in New York, including leading writers, intellectuals, and musicians. Writers Maya Angelou and Toni Morrison gave eulogies. Morrison said that Baldwin gave her the gifts of language, courage, and vulnerability. However, in two hours of praise and remembrance, there was not one mention of Baldwin being gay. The only white speaker was the French ambassador, who pointed out that only France had awarded a high honor to Baldwin.

BALDWIN'S LEGACY

Baldwin's obituaries spoke highly of his legacy of

James Baldwin is remembered for his skill and courage in addressing the controversial topics of racial bigotry and homosexuality.

writing about civil rights. None mentioned his contributions toward acceptance of homosexuality. Baldwin critic Christopher Bram calls it the "degayification" of James Baldwin. He quotes a letter written to the *New York Times* that challenges the silence about Baldwin's sexuality. "For as a man and a writer, Baldwin was both black and gay, and in this combination he found his voice, his strength, and his crown." Bram concludes that many critics think it is too complicated to address both minority sides of him. They sacrificed the side that made them more uncomfortable.

Though he was one of the first American writers to write about homosexuality with honesty, Baldwin would not have thought of himself as a gay pioneer. He rejected labels that tried to reduce his experiences to a simplification. "I've loved a few men and I've loved a few women," was his most frequent response when asked about his sexuality, Campbell writes. In *The Price of a Ticket*, Baldwin explains, "There is nothing in me that is not in everybody else." He thought that each of us contains the other, "male in female, female in male, white in black, and black in white." Ultimately, he says, we are part of each other.

James Baldwin's life was full of struggle. He had much success, but that brought him no relief from prejudice. He experienced disappointments

that plunged him into depression and despair.
His writing helped people, both black and white,
see what they had not seen before. His books
persuaded them toward a greater understand-
ing of themselves and the racist society in which
they lived. His message was consistent. Prejudice
inspires hatred, and the victims of this hatred
have been both black and gay. The solution
is not violence. For Baldwin, the solution was
always love.

TIMELINE

1924 James Arthur Baldwin is born on August 2 in Harlem, New York.

1935 Baldwin enters Frederick Douglass Junior High, where he is influenced by teacher and literary club adviser Countee Cullen, a leading poet of the Harlem Renaissance.

1938 Baldwin, age fourteen, joins the Fireside Pentecostal Assembly and becomes a preacher. He enters DeWitt Clinton High School in the Bronx.

1942 Baldwin graduates from high school and renounces the ministry. He leaves home to work for the New Jersey railroad.

1943 Baldwin's stepfather, David Baldwin, dies of tuberculosis.

1944 Baldwin meets novelist Richard Wright in Greenwich Village.

1945 Baldwin receives a $500 grant from *Harper's* magazine's Eugene F. Saxton Memorial Trust.

1947 Baldwin's first professional publication, the review "Gorky as an Artist," appears in the *Nation* magazine.

1948 Baldwin moves to Paris, France.

1953 Baldwin's first novel, *Go Tell It on the Mountain*, is published by Knopf and receives critical praise.

1954 Baldwin wins a Guggenheim Fellowship. He completes his first play, *The Amen Corner*.

1955 Baldwin's first collection of essays, *Notes of a Native Son*, is published.

1956 Baldwin's second novel, *Giovanni's Room*, is rejected by Knopf because of its subject. It is published by Dial.

1957 Baldwin returns to the United States to participate in the civil rights movement and meets Martin Luther King Jr.

1961 Baldwin's second collection of essays, *Nobody Knows My Name*, is published by Dial.

1962 Baldwin's novel *Another Country* is published by Dial and becomes a national bestseller. He meets Elijah Muhammad of the Nation of Islam.

1963 Baldwin's book *The Fire Next Time* is published. He meets with U.S. Attorney General Robert F. Kennedy. Baldwin is the subject of *Time* magazine's cover story.

1964 Baldwin's second play, *Blues for Mr. Charlie*, is published by Dial and produced by a theater in New York. He participates in a civil rights march from Selma to Montgomery, Alabama.

1965 *Going to Meet the Man*, a collection of short stories, is published by Dial.

1968 The novel *Tell Me How Long the Train's Been Gone* is published by Dial.

1972 *No Name in the Street*, an essay about the civil rights movement, is published.

1974 Baldwin's fifth novel, *If Beale Street Could Talk*, is published.

1976 Baldwin's first children's book, *Little Man, Little Man: A Story of Childhood*, is published by Dial.

1978 Baldwin begins teaching literature courses at Bowling Green State University in Ohio. He is awarded the Martin Luther King Memorial Medal for lifelong dedication to humanitarian ideals at City College of New York.

1979 Baldwin publishes his last novel, *Just Above My Head*.

1983 Baldwin becomes a Professor of Literature and Afro-American Studies at the Five College Network in Massachusetts.

1985 *The Price of the Ticket: Collected Non-Fiction, 1948–1985* is published by St. Martin's Press.

1986 Baldwin is awarded France's highest honor, the Legion of Honor.

1987 Baldwin dies of cancer on December 1.

ACCOLADES Marks of recognition of merit; praise.

AMBIVALENT Having attitudes that contradict each other.

ANTIDOTE Something that counteracts the harmful effects of something.

BANALITY Lacking originality, freshness, or novelty; trite.

CHALET A cottage or small house, often in vacation areas of the Alps.

CIVIL RIGHTS The rights of personal liberty, regardless of race, sex, or religion.

CONFISCATE To take away someone's property, often done by the government.

CRUCIBLE A situation that forces people to change or make difficult decisions.

DEFERMENT An official postponement of military service.

DESEGREGATE To eliminate policies of segregation, the isolation of races.

DEVIANT Different from what is considered to be normal or morally correct.

EULOGY A speech written in honor of one who has died.

EXPATRIATE To withdraw from residence in one's native country.

EXUBERANCE The state of being joyously unrestrained and enthusiastic.

GRATUITOUS Not involving a return benefit or compensation.

INITIATION The process of being formally accepted as a member of a group or organization.

JIM CROW Discrimination against blacks by law enforcement based on written and unwritten laws, primarily in the South.

KU KLUX KLAN A secret society that advocates white supremacy and that routinely terrorized blacks in the South.

LYNCHING Putting to death (as by hanging) by mob action without legal sanction.

MIGRANT A person who travels from one place to another to find work.

MILITANCY The use of extreme methods to achieve a goal.

MISCEGENATION Marriage between a white person and a person of another race.

OBSCENE Shocking or morally questionable.

OSTRACIZED To be excluded from a group.

PENTECOSTAL Evangelical Christian group that emphasizes a personal experience with God through baptism of the holy spirit.

PINNACLE The point of greatest success or achievement.

PREJUDICE Unfair or unaccounted for dislike of a person or group, based only on race, ethnicity, sex, or religion.

RATION To control the amount of something, especially when it is in short supply.

RETRACTION A statement saying that something one wrote at an earlier time is not true or correct.

SCAPEGOAT A person who is irrationally blamed, often with great hostility, for others.

SCRUTINY The act of carefully examining something, especially in a critical way.

SEGREGATE To separate racial groups.

SIT-IN A form of protest involving occupation of an area until demands are met.

SUBSERVIENT Less important than something or someone else.

SUBVERSION An attempt to undermine a government by working secretly from within.

TUBERCULOSIS A communicable disease that primarily affects the lungs.

VERNACULAR Using the language of ordinary speech, rather than formal writing.

Advocates for Youth
2000 M Street NW, Suite 75
Washington, DC 20036
(202) 419-3420
Website: http://www.advocatesforyouth.org
Advocates for Youth champions efforts to help young
people make informed and responsible decisions
about their reproductive and sexual health.

Egale: Canada Human Rights Trust
185 Carlton Street
Toronto, ON M5A 2K7
Canada
(416) 964-7887
Website: http://www.egale.ca
Egale promotes lesbian, gay, bisexual, trans, and
questioning (LGBT) human rights through
research, education, and community engagement.
It provides resources and a website for Canada's
lesbian, gay, bisexual, trans, and queer-question-
ing (LGBT) communities.

Gay Lesbian Straight Education Network (GLSEN)
90 Broad Street, 2nd Floor
New York, NY 10004
(212) 727-0135
Website: http://www.glesn.org
GLSEN works to ensure that LGBT students are able

to learn and grow in a school environment free from bullying and harassment. It provides research and resources for students, educators, and parents.

GLBT National Help Center
2261 Market Street, PMB #296
San Francisco, CA 94114
(415) 355-0003
Website: http://www.glbtnationalhelpcenter.org
The GLBT National Help Center is a nonprofit organization that is dedicated to meeting the needs of the gay, lesbian, bisexual, and transgender community and those questioning their sexual orientation and gender identity.

Human Rights Campaign (HRC)
1640 Rhode Island Avenue NW
Washington, DC 20036-3278
(202) 628-4160
Website: http://www.hrc.org
HRC advocates on behalf of LGBT Americans, mobilizes grassroots actions in diverse communities, invests strategically to elect fair-minded individuals to office, and educates the public about LGBT issues.

It Gets Better Project
110 S. Fairfax Avenue, Suite A11-71

Los Angeles, CA 90036

Website: http://www.itgetsbetter.org

The It Gets Better Project's mission is to communi-
cate to lesbian, gay, bisexual, and transgender
youth around the world that it gets better, and to
create and inspire the changes needed to make
life better for them.

James Baldwin Photographs and Papers

Beinecke Rare Book & Manuscript Library

121 Wall Street

New Haven, CT 06511

(203) 432-2977

Website: http://beinecke.library.yale.edu/collections/
highlights/james-baldwin-photographs-and-papers

The Beinecke Rare Book & Manuscript Library at Yale
University houses manuscripts, photographs, and
correspondence that document the career of James
Baldwin. Selected correspondence and early drafts
of *Go Tell It on the Mountain* are available online.

Live Out Loud

570 7th Avenue, 9th Floor

New York, NY 10018

(212) 651-4236

Website: http://www.liveoutloud.info/wp

Live Out Loud is a nonprofit organization dedicated
to inspiring and empowering LGBT youth by

connecting them with successful LGBT profes-
sionals in their community.

Point Foundation
5757 Wilshire Boulevard, Suite 370
Los Angeles, CA 90036
(866) 337-6468
Website: http://www.pointfoundation.org
The Point Foundation offers mentorship, leadership
development, and community service training to
lesbian, gay, bisexual, transgender, and queer
(LGBTQ) students.

Pride Education Network
Box 93678, Nelson Park PO
Vancouver, BC V6E 4L7
Canada
Website: http://pridenet.ca
The Pride Education Network of teachers, adminis-
trators, support staff, youth, and parents strives
to make the British Columbia school system
more welcoming and equitable for LGBTQ stu-
dents, staff, and queer families.

The Trevor Project
P.O. Box 69232
West Hollywood, CA 90069
(866) 488-7386

Website: http://www.thetrevorproject.org

The Trevor Project is a national organization that provides crisis intervention and suicide prevention services to lesbian, gay, bisexual, transgender, and questioning youth.

WEBSITES

Because of the changing nature of Internet links, Rosen Publishing has developed an online list of websites related to the subject of this book. This site is updated regularly. Please use this link to access the list:

http://www.rosenlinks.com/LGBT/Bald

FOR FURTHER READING

Baldwin, James. *Giovanni's Room.* New York, NY: Delta, 1956.

Bronkski, Michael. *A Queer History of the United States.* Boston, MA: Beacon Press, 2011.

Carbado, Devon W., Dwight A. McBride, and Donald Weise. *Black Like Us: A Century of Lesbian, Gay and Bisexual African American Fiction.* San Francisco, CA: Cleis Press, 2002.

Cart, Michael, and Christine A. Jenkins. *The Heart Has Its Reasons: Young Adult Literature with Gay/Lesbian/Queer Content, 1969–2004.* Lanham, MA: Scarecrow Publishing, 2012.

Cleaver, Eldridge. *Soul on Ice.* New York, NY: McGraw-Hill, 1964.

Elledge, Jim, and David Groff, eds. *Who's Yer Daddy? Gay Writers Celebrate Their Mentors and Forerunners.* Madison, WI: University of Wisconsin Press, 2012.

Garden, Nancy. *Hear Us Out: Lesbian and Gay Stories of Progress and Hope, 1950 to the Present.* New York, NY: Farrar, Straus and Giroux, 2007.

Gay, Kathlyn. *Bigotry and Intolerance: The Ultimate Teen Guide* (It Happened to Me). Lanham, MA: Scarecrow Press, 2013.

Harris, E. Lynn. *Freedom in this Village: Twenty-Five Years of Black Gay Men's Writing.* New York, NY: Carroll & Graf Publishers, 2005.

Johnson, David K. *The Lavender Scare: The Cold War Persecution of Gays and Lesbians in the Federal Government.* Chicago, IL: University of Chicago Press, 2006.

Kuhn, Betsy. *Gay Power! The Stonewall Riots and the Gay Rights Movement, 1969* (Civil Rights Struggles Around the World). Minneapolis, MN: Twenty-First Century Books, 2011.

Loftin, Craig. Letters to One: Gay and Lesbian Voices from the 1950s and 1960s. Albany, NY: State University of New York Press, 2012.

Malcolm X and Alex Haley. *The Autobiography of Malcolm X.* New York, NY: Ballantine Publishing Group, 1964.

Mobly-Till, Mamie, and Christopher Benson. *Death of Innocence: The Story of the Hate Crime that Changed America.* New York, NY: One World, 2003.

Mogul, Joey, Andrea J. Ritchie, and Kay Whitlock. *Queer (In)Justice: The Criminalization of LGBT People in the United States.* Boston, MA: Beacon Press, 2012.

Sadowski, Michael. *In a Queer Voice: Journeys of Resilience from Adolescence to Adulthood.* Philadelphia, PA: Temple University, 2013.

Schwartz, Christa. *Gay Voices of the Harlem Renaissance.* Bloomington, IN: Indiana University Press, 2003.

Setterington, Ken. *Branded by the Pink Triangle.* Toronto, ON, Canada: Second Story Press, 2013.

Webber, Carlisle K. *Gay, Lesbian, Bisexual, Transgender and Questioning Teen Literature: a Guide to Reading Interests.* Santa Barbara, CA: Libraries Unlimited, 2010.

Wright, Simeon. *Simeon's Story: An Eyewitness Account of the Kidnapping of Emmett Till.* Chicago, IL: Chicago Review Press, 2011.

American Civil Liberties Union. "Governor Mifflin
    School District and Filtering of LGBT Online
    Content." February 27, 2013. Retrieved
    December 10, 2013 (https://www.aclu.org/
    free-speech-lgbt-rights/governor-mifflin-school
    -district-and-filtering-lgbt-online-content).
Baldwin, James. *Collected Essays*. New York, NY:
    Library of America, 1998.
Baldwin, James. *The Fire Next Time*. New York,
    NY: Vintage, 1993.
Baldwin, James. "If Black English Isn't a
    Language, Then Tell Me, What Is?" *New York
    Times*, July 29, 1979.
Baldwin, James. *Nobody Knows My Name*. New
    York, NY: Dial, 1961.
Baldwin, James. *No Name in the Street*. New
    York, NY: Dial, 1972.
Baldwin, James. *Notes of a Native Son*. Boston,
    MA: Beacon Press, 1983.
Baldwin, James. *The Price of a Ticket*. New York,
    NY: St. Martin's Press, 1985.
Bram, Christopher. *Eminent Outlaws: The Gay
    Writers Who Changed America*. New York, NY:
    Hachette Book Group, 2012.
Campbell, James. *Talking at the Gates: A Life of
    James Baldwin*. Berkeley, CA: University of
    California Press, 1991.
Clark, Keith. *Black Manhood in James Baldwin,
    Ernest J. Gaines, and August Wilson*.
    Champaign, IL: University of Illinois
    Press, 2004.

Cleaver, Eldridge. "Notes of a Native Son."
    Ramparts, June 1966. Retrieved January 3,
    2013 (http://www.unz.org/Pub/Ramparts
    -1966jun-00051).
Daily, Peter. "Jimmy." *American Scholar*, Winter
    1994: 102–111.
Gay, Lesbian & Straight Education Network. "LGBT
    Students Experience Pervasive Harassment,
    But School-Based Resourcees and Supports
    Are Making a Difference." National School
    Climate Survey, 2003–2012. Retrieved
    December 10, 2013 (http://www.glsen.org
    /schoolclimate).
Goldberg, Beverly. "Utah Suit Restores Access to
    In Our Mothers' House." *American Libraries*,
    Mar/Apr 2013: 11.
Gottfried, Ted. James Baldwin. New York, NY:
    Franklin Watts, 1997.
Kenan, Randall. *James Baldwin* (Lives of Notable
    Gay Men and Lesbians). New York, NY:
    Chelsea House Publishing, 1994.
Kenan, Randall, and Amy Sickels. James
    Baldwin. New York, NY: Chelsea House
    Publishing, 2005.
Leeming, David. *James Baldwin: A Biography.*
    New York, NY: Knopf, 1994.
National Public Radio. "American Lives: James
    Baldwin, 'Lifting the Veil.'" August 19,
    2010. Retrieved December 18, 2013
    (http://www.npr.org/templates/story/story
    .php?storyId=129281259).

PBS.org. "Why Did the Mafia Own the Bar?" *American Experience: Stonewall Uprising.* 2011. Retrieved January 3, 2013 (http://www.pbs.org/wgbh/americanexperience/features/general-article/stonewall-mafia).

Rosset, Lisa. *James Baldwin.* New York, NY: Chelsea House Publishers, 1989.

Shin, Andrew, and Barbara Judson. "Beneath the Black Aesthetic: James Baldwin's Primer of Black American Masculinity." African American Review, Vol. 32, Issue 2 (1998): 247–261.

Weatherby, James J. *James Baldwin: Artist on Fire.* New York, NY: Dutton, 1989.

INDEX

ABOUT THE AUTHOR

Susan Henneberg has been a literature teacher at the high school and college level in Reno, Nevada, for more than thirty years. As an advocate for youth, she has worked with at-risk populations to provide physical, emotional, and academic support to help all students achieve their goals. A particular interest has been supporting young writers in self-expression through poetry, fiction, and film. She has written numerous young adult nonfiction books.

PHOTO CREDITS